DOES YOUR DNA
CREATE WEALTH?

LIFESUCCESS PUBLISHING, LLC
8900 E Pinnacle Peak Road, Suite D240
Scottsdale, AZ 85255

Telephone:	800.473.7134
Fax:	480.661.1014
E-mail:	admin@lifesuccesspublishing.com
Cover & Layout:	Lloyd Arbour & LifeSuccess Publishing

COMPANIES, ORGANIZATIONS, INSTITUTIONS, AND INDUSTRY PUBLICATIONS: Quantity discounts are available on bulk purchases of this book for reselling, educational purposes, subscription incentives, gifts, sponsorship, or fundraising. Special books or book excerpts can also be created to fit specific needs such as private labeling with your logo on the cover and a message from a VIP printed inside. For more information please contact our Special Sales Department at LifeSuccess Publishing.

This publication is designed to provide accurate and authoritative information in reagard to the subject matter covered. It is sold with the understanding that neither the author nor the publisher is engaged in rendering legal, accounting, or other professional service. If legal advice or other expert assistance is required, the services of a competent professional person should be sought.

DOES YOUR DNA CREATE WEALTH?

LINDA PROCTOR

THIS BOOK IS DEDICATED TO EVERYONE WHO HAS A SINCERE DESIRE TO IMPROVE THEIR RESULTS.

TABLE OF CONTENTS

ACKNOWLEDGMENTS

I would like to thank Mr. Gerry Robert and the staff at LifeSuccess Publishing for all their assistance in making this book a reality.

Last but not least, I would like to thank the man who inspired me to never stop reaching for the top, and without whose support and encouragement, this book would not have been possible – my husband Bob Proctor.

FOREWORD

There are many lessons we can learn in life. Each day we are confronted with a problem. Instead of getting discouraged, we should train our minds to look at this obstacle as a lesson.

Linda Proctor learned a very valuable lesson, and she's sharing it in her book *Does Your DNA Create Wealth?* Linda learned that while she enjoyed making big money that made her life comfortable, she had no time left for herself, or her family. She felt chained to her job. Linda knew she wanted to maintain her lifestyle, yet be able to work from anywhere in the world, on her own time, without any employees. Most thought Linda's wish was ridiculous. But Linda put her plan into action and achieved her goal.

I've had the privilege of knowing Linda for more than 20 years. I've watched this determined woman do what was necessary to make her life the one she wanted. Linda is a living example of what each and everyone of us can have, if we change the way we have been conditioned to think.

I assure you that even as you begin to read *Does Your DNA Create Wealth?* you will start to see how your years of conditioning to work a certain way, have held you back from achieving what you really want.

In my book *The Millionaire Mindset*, I talk about the philosophies of wealthy people and how an ordinary person from an average or impoverished background (like me) can acquire a wealthy mindset and transform the financial pattern of their family tree forever.

Linda also began her adult life with hardships. She married young, and 18 months into her marriage her husband was diagnosed with terminal cancer. He passed away 18 months later. Linda was making enough money to get by, but maintained a burning passion to make much more. A passion lead her to attend a seminar by Bob Proctor, author of *You Were Born Rich*, and star of the hit movie *The Secret*. Bob told her, *"Linda, if you can tell me what you want, I can show you how to get it."* It was not only an eye-opening experience for Linda, it was an encounter that would eventually lead her down the aisle, with Bob as her new husband.

Does Your DNA Create Wealth? is not just an incredible story of a woman who wrote down her life plan, followed the route, and made it to her destination. It's a step-by-step guide on what necessary changes you need to make, to live the life you've always wanted.

I'm proud of what Linda has achieved, and thankful she has written this book, to help others get started on the road to their dream life.

– Gerry Robert,
Bestselling author of *The Millionaire Mindset*
www.gerryrobert.com

CHAPTER 1

MY ROAD TO RICHES

My Road To Riches

I am just one of a very large group of people scattered all around the world who frequently count their blessings that they met Bob Proctor. Bob has changed the lives of countless thousands of people in many different ways, but he totally changed the direction of my life when he became my husband. And now through the run-away bestselling movie *The Secret*, in which Bob is featured, he is impacting the lives of millions of people all around the world.

Bob Proctor is a unique coach and mentor. He is able to help individuals set and achieve extraordinary goals. A number of years ago I was working with an individual who was struggling. It was then I realized, that what Bob had taught me, I was able to teach others. The information that transformed my life... was transferable. Let me explain.

When I first met Bob Proctor in 1979 I was struggling in sales and had been struggling for over three years. However, Bob saw in me something I could not see. In a quiet, clear conversation, he explained a few fascinating facts about my potential that I had never heard before. He then said, *"Linda, if you can tell me what you want, I can show you how to get it."* He actually got me excited about myself, my potential, and what I was capable of accomplishing.

He explained that everyone is hardwired to do what they are doing, to get the results they are getting. He said that is precisely why people have difficulty making any dramatic or consistent change in their results. He said that your DNA will either create wealth or it will not; you have to take an honest look at your results and you will see exactly what you are hardwired to

do. He said, *"Contrary to popular belief, your DNA can be changed. If you want your DNA to create wealth, I can explain exactly what you have to do."*

He went on to explain that he had done it many years before when he took his own income from $4,000 a year to over a million. He explained that he still wasn't satisfied with the change he made because he wanted to know why… he wanted to know what happened to him. And since that is what he was looking for, that is what he found. He had altered his paradigm, his conditioning, or as he stated, his DNA. He said that it took nine years of intensive research but he proved to himself, beyond a shadow of a doubt, that anyone can alter their DNA and create wealth in their life with the proper information and a total commitment to do so.

I made up my mind then and there that if he could show me what to do, I would definitely commit to do it. The various chapters in this book cover point by point, the lessons that he shared with me; lessons that took me from a struggling mediocre salesperson, to one of the top producers in my industry.

If you will make the same decision now as I made then, I can guarantee that wealth will not be a visitor but will take up permanent residence in your life. But before I get into the lessons let me share with you where I was and what happened.

Here is how it began for me… In 1979 I met Bob Proctor at a seminar. It was clearly a turning point, both the seminar and meeting Bob.

I had married right out of university. Eighteen months into that marriage my husband was diagnosed with terminal cancer and passed away eighteen months later.

During the three years we were together we created a lifestyle which was quite comfortable based on two salaries. But now that he was gone I had to make a decision... develop a lifestyle that could be sustained on my salary only, or increase my income so that I did not have to change the lifestyle to which I had become accustomed.

I had either read or heard that selling was the highest paid profession in the world. Since my husband had been in sales... and did well... I believed that sales would be the vehicle that could provide me with the income I needed. And so I started interviewing for sales positions.

I can't tell you how many companies I interviewed with, I only know there were many. And everyone, without exception, gave me an aptitude test... the results came back... no sales aptitude... and I was encouraged to stay where I was.

Looking back years later, I realized that in my search for a sales position I was learning to deal with something all great salespeople deal with – rejection – and I was not letting it stop me.

Finally a female sales manager in a life insurance company offered me a sales position... straight commission! I was enthusiastic because I really saw sales as the vehicle to change my life!

It's interesting... when I shared with friends and family that I had secured a sales job, most of their comments were discouraging, and when they found out it was selling life insurance... well, they quickly let me know not to phone them!

It seemed the only person enthusiastic about what I was doing was me. Looking back I realized that was all that was

necessary. This deal was strictly between me and myself and I had made the decision I was going to learn how to sell.

Three years into my sales career in the insurance industry, I found myself at a Bob Proctor Seminar! I was earning $25,000 a year and needing to earn much more. I was struggling and frustrated. Let me put the numbers into perspective for you... I would cold call 200 people a week and would generally secure 10 appointments. Once every three weeks I would make a sale. Not great percentages... I knew it and my managers knew it.

When I shared these statistics with Bob, I clearly remember that all he did was smile and said, "Linda, I work with a different strategy. I make one call and sell 200 people." But I'm getting ahead of myself... let's go back to the seminar.

Bob stood in the front of the room and asked us if we could see ourselves earning $100,000 a year. The only thoughts running through my mind were that I could see myself spending it, but with my track record, I was having a lot of difficulty seeing myself earning it.

Then came our first personal encounter. Bob took the time to sit down with me. He was the first person who asked me what I really wanted... how I really wanted to be living. I quickly learned from him that if you are ever going to get a person to dramatically improve their results, you must find out what they want. From that point on you never talk about their results, you talk to them about what they want. Assure them that you can help them get what they want. It's WANTS that motivate people, that inspire them to reach a little higher and run a little faster... sell a little more.

He told me that he could show me how to achieve that lifestyle and asked me to commit to doing two things. I wanted

13

to know what they were; I wanted to be sure that they were moral and ethical. He asked me if I would:

> 1. Commit to being in front of a prospect every morning by 9 a.m.
>
> 2. Ask everyone I speak with to purchase $100,000 of life insurance.

I MADE THE COMMITMENT

I made the commitment to Bob that I would do these two things, and in turn, he would hold me accountable. (I not only wanted to win, I wanted to impress him). Then I thought about the commitment I had made and I suddenly became very nervous. I could feel panic setting in. I had been in sales for over three years, I knew how to do things. The problem? I wasn't doing them. In fact, in the three years I had been in the business, I can't ever remember having an appointment before 9 a.m.

Bob explained that if a person's compensation is on commission and they are not in front of a prospect, they are unemployed. It doesn't matter how busy the salesperson is doing other THINGS related to the job, they must get in front of prospects.

I rationalized that these two items seemed too simple to make a profound difference in my results, although I did believe they would make an impact. I believed that to make a big difference in my results, I had to make a big difference in the activity. How wrong I was. *Small changes can make a Big difference.* A little over a year later I was earning close to $500,000!

The 9 a.m. call and the $100,000 sale idea was the first step in a series of lessons that Bob taught me. I have outlined all the lessons in this book, and for close to 30 years, these lessons have kept me at the top of my profession. These same lessons will reward you exactly the same way.

Bob and I went on to become husband and wife. In the mid '80s, at Bob's encouragement, I started my own financial services company and did very well. However, that company, and the responsibility that came with it, was very demanding of my time. I wanted freedom... time freedom. I already enjoyed money freedom. Therefore, I sold the business.

Again, Bob said, if you know what you want, write it on a sheet of paper and ask yourself how to get it. I wrote that I wanted to have my own business with no limit on income. I did not want to have any employees nor did I want to have an office. I wanted to be able to operate my business from anywhere in the world... to have the freedom to come and go as I pleased. Bob looked at it and smiled. Again he said, *"You are going to have to change your DNA because right now you are hardwired to work the way you have always been working. You are going to have to look in an unconventional place for something that is unconventional. But understand this – if you are able to think it, you can most certainly do it."* And I have been in that business for the past 12 years.

If a business like that sounds appealing to you, I can help you get it. **www.lindaproctor.com**

And now I can honestly tell you that if you can tell me what you want, I can show you how to get it. I have learned how to transfer the information that Bob gave me to others and I have helped a lot of people earn a lot of money. I would enjoy helping you!

"GOD HAS ENTRUSTED
ME WITH MYSELF."

– EPICTETUS, GREEK PHILOSOPHER
C.50 – C.125 A.D.

CHAPTER 2

MULTIPLE SOURCES OF INCOME

DNA STRAND 1:

MULTIPLE SOURCES OF INCOME

"The good life is expensive. There is another way to live that doesn't cost as much but it isn't any good."

– Spanish Distiller

> **Are you serious about wanting to earn a lot of money?**
>
> **Do you want to live the good life that the Spanish Distiller referred to?**

I am going to proceed on the premise that you answered yes to both of those questions; an emphatic YES. And I am going to share a fundamental principle that all wealthy people follow. All wealthy people have Multiple Sources of Income (M.S.I.). Some are large, some are small… and they are forever setting up New Sources of Income.

To wealthy people, earning money is a game; a game that permits them to continually work at developing their creative abilities. They know they can improve. You could compare it to golf… no one has ever shot 18. The best players in the world know they can play a better game and they are forever attempting to do so.

You cannot have too many sources of income, but you can most certainly have too few. Unfortunately most people have been raised to believe that you live on one source of income... hopefully a good one. Adopt the idea, RIGHT NOW, that you can have thousands of sources of income.

Creating wealth the M.S.I. way is a relatively easy process and can be a lot of fun. It can turn your days into an exciting adventure. What all thinking people want (and I'm tossing you into that category) is financial independence, financial and emotional well-being. The remainder of this MSI chapter contains some of the most important information you will ever study.

MSI TECHNOLOGY

Multiple Sources of Income is a technology which will permit you to multiply your present income, by providing service beyond that which you are currently providing at your primary source of income.

Your P.S.I. (Primary Source of Income), could be your job. You might be able to create an M.S.I. from your P.S.I. but you want to get income coming to you from various sources. For example, if you are in insurance, you could create additional income from this business by giving lectures, training other agents, or doing joint ventures with professionals in other non-competing professions.

M1, M2 AND M3 ARE THREE WAYS OF EARNING MONEY!

M1 (Money 1), is the way 96% of the population earn their income; they are trading time for money. And when you run out of time... you run out of the ability to earn any more income. When I was in life insurance sales and even when I owned my financial services company... I was practicing M1. With each move, each advancement, I was able to make more money for the time I put in... but I still had to put in time.

Michael Gerber wrote a book called the *E-Myth* and in it he says: *"If your business requires your presence, you don't have a business, you have a job."* And that's exactly where I was... working 70, 80 sometimes 90 hours per week.

M2 (Money 2) is the way 3% of the population earns their income... they invest money to earn money. This is a great way, if you have the assets and the skill. However, it can be difficult to accumulate the assets if earning in the M1 strategy.

M3 (Money 3) is by far the best way of earning money. This is where you leverage yourself... through multiple sources of income. This is the way 1% of the population earns their income... but this group earns 96% of the money.

A traditional example would be the person who starts a franchise. As the franchise gets off the ground... franchisees coming on board... product or services being sold... money is coming in from many sources and is not dependant on the activity of the individual, or individuals, who own the business. This is leveraging.

* * *

A little over 10 years ago I found myself on a treadmill and didn't know how to get off. I was making excellent money but working long, long hours. I wanted a career… but I wanted it on my terms. I went to Bob and asked for his advice. He suggested that I explore network marketing. He told me it was one of the best ways he knew of creating multiple sources of income. He said that if I truly wanted time and money freedom, that was the industry for me.

I did check it out and have spent the last 12 years in the industry. I have earned millions and compared to my prior workloads, I have barely worked!

Through M.S.I. Technology you will earn many times what you are currently earning at your primary source of income. M.S.I. is a concept which has been adopted by almost all very wealthy people. Multiple Sources of Income is exactly what it says… it is:

INCOME FROM MULTIPLE SOURCES.

> M.S.I. is not another JOB.
>
> M.S.I. is not a better JOB.
>
> M.S.I. is not even a JOB.

M.S.I. is a way of adding a new dimension of excitement and fun to your everyday life, while you are becoming very wealthy. An M.S.I. is an idea that you are in harmony with. An M.S.I. is an idea which enables you to provide service to humanity in a lawful manner for which you will be fairly

compensated. The compensation you receive from each M.S.I. could be minimal or it could be millions of dollars per year.

An M.S.I. should not interfere with, nor cause you to jeopardize, your position at your primary source of income.

> *"Never before in the history of the world have so many people had the opportunity to be wealthy beyond their wildest dreams."*
>
> – Tod Barnhart

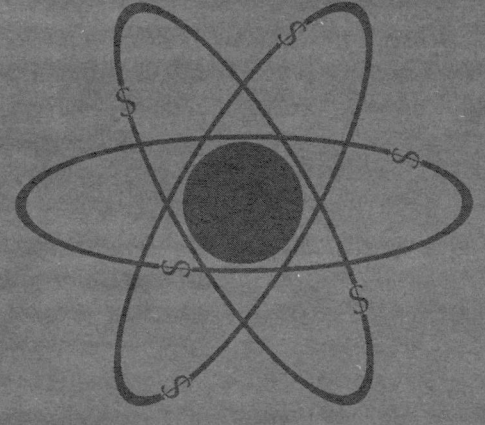

CHAPTER 3

DECISION

DNA STRAND 2:

DECISION

There is a single mental move you can make which, in a millisecond, will solve enormous problems for you. It has the potential to improve almost any personal or business situation you will ever encounter... and it could literally propel you down the path to incredible success. We have a name for this magic mental activity... it is called

"DECISION."

The world's most successful people share a common quality – they make decisions. Yes, decision makers go to the top and those who do not make decisions seem to go nowhere. THINK ABOUT IT.

Decisions, or the lack of them, are responsible for the making or breaking of careers. Individuals who have become very proficient at making decisions, without being influenced by the opinions of others, are the same people whose annual incomes fall into the six and seven figure category. The person who has never developed the strength to make these mental moves is relegated to the lower income ranks their entire commercial career. *The DNA of Wealth* is something they would probably believe is a special gift from a capricious God. More often than not, their life becomes little more than a dull, boring existence. Their creative faculties have probably never been exercised.

It is not just your income that is affected by decisions... your whole life is dominated by this power. The health of your mind and body, the well-being of your family, your social life, the type of relationships you develop, are all dependent upon your ability to make sound decisions.

At this point you could be asking yourself, *"How is a person expected to develop this mental ability?"* Well... I have the answer for you. You must do it on your own and you have already begun by thinking about and digesting this information that I am sharing with you. This chapter is causing you to become more aware of the importance of decisions.

You can virtually eliminate conflict and confusion in your life by becoming proficient at making decisions. Decision making brings order to your mind... and of course, this order is then reflected in your objective world... your results. James Allen, the great Victorian author, might have been thinking of decision when he wrote, *"We think in secret and it comes to pass. Environment is but our looking glass."* No one can see you making decisions but they almost always see the results of your decisions. The person who fails to develop their ability to make decisions is doomed because indecision sets up internal conflicts, which can, without warning, escalate into all-out mental and emotional wars. Psychiatrists have a name to describe these internal wars; it is AMBIVALENCE. My Oxford Dictionary tells me that ambivalence is the co-existence, in one person, of opposite feelings towards the same objective.

Everyone on occasion has had feelings of ambivalence. If it happens too frequently, decide right now to stop it. The cause of ambivalence is indecision, but we must keep in mind that the truth is not always in the appearance of things. Indecision may be a cause of ambivalence, however it is a secondary cause, it is not a primary cause. People who have become very proficient at making decisions have one thing in common. They have a very strong self-image, and a high degree of self-esteem. They may be as different as night is to day in numerous other respects, but they certainly possess confidence. Low self-esteem or a lack of confidence is the real culprit here. Decision makers are not afraid of making an error. If and when they make an error in their decision, or fail at something, they have the ability to shrug it off. They learn from experience but they never submit to failure.

Every decision maker was either fortunate enough to have been raised in an environment where decision making was part of their upbringing, or they developed the ability themselves at a later date. They are aware of something that everyone, who hopes to live a full life, must understand: decision making is something you cannot avoid. You may be thinking, *"Alright, where do I start?"* You start right here… right now… send an e-mail to me, **linda@lindaproctor.com,** and just tell me that you have made your decision… you want to create wealth.

You start improving your ability to make decisions in exactly the same place you start any journey and with exactly the same resources. You decide. Start right where you are with whatever you've got. That is the cardinal principle of decision making. DECIDE RIGHT WHERE YOU ARE WITH WHATEVER YOU'VE GOT. This is precisely why most people never master this important aspect of life. They permit their resources to dictate if and when a decision will or can be made. When John Kennedy asked Werner Von Braun what it would take to build a rocket that would carry a man to the moon and return him safely to earth, Von Braun's answer was simple and direct. *"The will to do it."* President Kennedy never asked if it was possible. He never asked if they could afford it, or any one of a thousand other questions, all of which would have… at the time… been valid questions.

President Kennedy made a decision. He said, *"We will put a man on the moon and return him safely to earth before the end of the decade."* That it had never been done before in all the hundreds of thousands of years of human history was not even a consideration. He DECIDED where he was with what he had. The objective was accomplished in his mind the second he made the decision. It was only a matter of time, which is governed by natural law, before the goal was manifested in the physical or material form for the whole world to see.

Thinking is very important. Decision makers are great thinkers. Do you ever give much consideration to your thoughts and how they affect the various aspects of your life? Although this should be one of our most serious considerations, unfortunately, for many people it is not. There are a select few who make any attempt to control or govern their thoughts.

Anyone who has made a study of the great thinkers, the great decision makers, the achievers of history, will know they very rarely agreed on anything when it came to the study of human life. However, there was one point on which they were in complete and unanimous agreement and that is, *"We become what we think about."*

What do you think about? You and I must realize that our thoughts ultimately control every decision we make. You are the sum total of your thoughts. By taking charge this very minute, you can guarantee yourself a good day. Refuse to let unhappy, negative people or circumstances affect you.

The greatest stumbling block you will encounter when making important decisions in your life is circumstance. We let circumstances get us off the hook when we should be giving it everything we've got. More dreams are shattered and goals lost because of circumstance than any other single factor.

How often have you caught yourself saying, *"I would like to do or have this but I can't because…"* Whatever follows *"because"* is the circumstance. Circumstances may cause a detour in your life but you should never permit them to stop you from making important decisions.

Napoleon said, *"Circumstance, I make them."*

The next time you hear someone say they would like a vacation in Paris, or want to purchase a particular automobile, but they can't because they have no money, explain they don't need the money until they have made a decision to go to Paris or purchase the car. When the decision is made, they will figure out a way to get the amount needed. They always do.

Many misguided individuals try something once or twice and if they do not hit the bull's-eye, they feel they are a failure. Failing does not make anyone a failure, but quitting most certainly does and quitting is a decision. By following that form of reasoning, you would have to say when you make a decision to quit, you make a decision to fail.

Charles F. Kettering said, *"When you're inventing, if you flunk 999 times and succeed once, you're in."* The world will soon forget your failures in light of your achievements. Don't worry about failing, it will toughen you up and get you ready for your big win. Winning is a decision.

Many years ago Helen Keller was asked if she thought there was anything worse than being blind. She quickly replied that there was something much worse. She said, *"The most pathetic person in the world is a person who has their sight but no vision."* I agree with Helen Keller.

At 91, J. C. Penny was asked how his eyesight was. He replied that his sight was failing but his vision had never been better. That is really great, isn't it? When your vision is clear it becomes easy to make decisions.

Take the first step in predicting your own prosperous future. Build a mental picture of exactly how you would like to live. Make a firm decision to hold on to that vision and positive ways to improve everything will begin to flow into your mind. In fact, e-mail me a written copy of your prosperity vision and if it needs an adjustment, I will make the necessary suggestions and send it right back to you.

Many people get a beautiful vision of how they would like to live or what they would like from their business, but because they cannot see how they are going to make it happen, they let the vision go. If they knew how they were going to get it or do it, they would have a plan, not a vision. There is no inspiration in a plan, but there sure is in a vision. When you get the vision, freeze-frame it in your mind with a decision and don't worry about how you will do it or where the resources will come from. Charge your decision with enthusiasm... that is important. Refuse to worry about how it will happen. There is a power much greater than you that never expresses itself other than perfectly, and it will take care of that responsibility.

There is no situation that isn't made worse by worry. Worry never solves anything. Worry never prevents anything. Worry never heals anything. Worry serves only one purpose... it makes matters worse.

James Kurtz said, *"If we worry, we don't trust; if we trust, we don't worry. Worry does not empty tomorrow of its grief, but it does empty today of its joy."*

Worrying about 'lack of' is a clear indication there is a serious misunderstanding with respect to our source of supply. By our source, I mean you and me. We are both receiving every good that comes into our life from the same source. There is only one source of supply. That is Spirit... everything comes from Spirit. When you clearly understand that, you will find making a decision is something easy to do.

When you truly understand the source of supply and then enhance your understanding with the law by which Spirit works, you will be able to make a decision and hold the picture of the successful outcome as a result of that decision... knowing that Spirit will instantly begin sending to you whatever you require for the manifestation of your picture.

I am well aware that there are millions of people who will laugh at you, if you attempted to get them to accept what I am saying. However, it is important for you to remember those same people are not able to explain why they are rejecting it or why it cannot happen.

I found an interesting idea that you can gain tremendous benefit from in your effort to become a more effective decision maker... Advanced Decision Making. Isn't that great? Think about it. We make advanced bookings when we fly somewhere, to eliminate any confusion or problems when time arrives for the journey. We do the same with renting a car, for the same reason. Think of the problems you will eliminate by making many of the decisions you must make... well in advance.

That same exact concept works with a person when they are on a diet to lose weight. Their decisions are made in advance. If they are offered a big slice of chocolate cake, they don't have to say, "*Gee, that looks good... I wonder if I should?*" The decision is made in advance.

I made a decision a long time ago that I would not participate in discussions of why something cannot be done. The only compensation you will ever receive for participating in, or giving energy to, that type of discussion is something you do not want. I always find it amazing at the number of seemingly intelligent people who persist in dragging you into these negative brainstorming sessions. In one breath, these people tell you they seriously want to accomplish a particular objective. And, in the next breath, they begin talking about why they can't. Think of how much more they would enjoy life by making a decision that they will no longer participate in that type of negative energy.

Permit me to caution you. Advance Decisions must be mixed with an ample supply of discipline. All peak performers understand and use discipline. Any decision you make must be backed by discipline. Research indicates that highly successful individuals make decisions very quickly and change those decisions very slowly, if and when they are changed at all. By comparison, the person who rarely enjoys any degree of success makes decisions very slowly and they change their decisions very quickly and often.

Those individuals who rarely win generally have the habit of being influenced in their decision making by the opinions of others; while their successful counterparts follow their own counsel. The most natural thing in the world for you to do in life is probably the most destructive, insofar as succeeding at anything is concerned – that 'thing' is *"following the crowd."* Historically, the crowd has always been traveling in the wrong direction.

You were encouraged to be like the other kids when you were young. You have been conditioned to follow the crowd. In many schools, you are even dressed like the other kids. Well, you're not a child any longer and you're not like the other kids. You are unique.

You may not have to go one page further if you have made Your Decision to create wealth immediately. Send me an e-mail: **Linda@lindaproctor.com** and I'll help you move as far and as fast as Bob helped me move. In fact, that's my business today... helping other people create wealth.

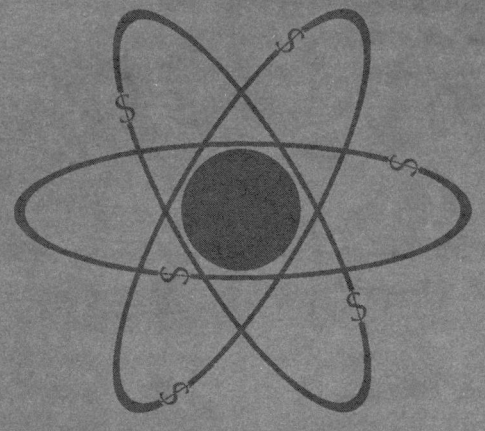

CHAPTER 4

RESPONSIBILITY

DNA STRAND 3:
RESPONSIBILITY

An absolute prerequisite for success in every aspect of your life is responsibility. Take this next statement, deposit it in the treasury of your subconscious mind… feel it… believe it and continually repeat it until it is a part of your genetic nature.

> *"I take complete and absolute responsibility for the results that I experience in all aspects of my life. Because I know I am responsible for what comes into my life, I daily train my mind to view everything that happens to me, for me or around me, as a lesson."*

Individuals who do not take responsibility for their results squander their potential. They rarely ever develop their higher faculties, thereby cheating themselves out of the good that could be theirs. Make certain that you do not fall into this category.

You have so much more potential than you can even imagine. Petite women have lifted cars, rich people have given everything away to serve as missionaries, poor people have become billionaires, and uneducated farmers have solved world crises. Anything is possible if you can persist and know how to get the most from yourself. You do that by… taking responsibility for your life.

PUT YOURSELF TOTALLY ON THE LINE EVERY TIME

The first element in putting yourself totally on the line every time you do something is to be wholly committed to yourself and to your activity. Until you are committed, there is room for hesitancy… that chance to draw back from progress. The result is always one of ineffectiveness. Steadfast resolution to put behind your effort everything you have – emotionally, mentally, and physically – without hesitation, is of critical importance. You must not let any fear of losing even enter your mind.

Failure does not exist! You may have some difficulty in rationalizing this concept, but all that is necessary is to view it from a different perspective than that with which you have been conditioned all your life.

> ### There are NO failures, only lessons!

Therefore, regardless of the outcome of your efforts, you still gain experience. You may not attain exactly what you had previously expected, in precisely the manner you intended, but you do gain knowledge. You still come out a winner, with success to build upon even further in the future. As long as you never give less than your best effort, the absolute minimum you will gain is self-satisfaction in having done your best.

Many times, we are afraid to take responsibility for our failures because failures often hurt. As a society, we have been wrongfully taught that failure is negative. Great achievers know that is not so. Thomas Edison tried 10,000 times before he discovered an electric light bulb that would work. While some would say he failed 10,000 times, Edison looked at it differently.

He said that he had discovered 10,000 ways that light bulbs would not work.

Henry Ford said, *"Failure is the opportunity to begin again more intelligently."* Babe Ruth is the Hall of Fame baseball player with the record for the most home runs, 714. He also has the world record for the greatest number of strikeouts – 1,330. Do you think there might be a correlation? Of course. If you fail twice as much, you will generally succeed twice as much, as long as you don't quit. Incidentally, which of Babe Ruth's records do you think he is best known for, his home runs or his strikeouts?

In the event that you do not attain your original goal immediately, refuse to make excuses. Reaffirm your commitment. There is a right time and place for everything.

NEVER SURRENDER

Never throw in the towel, even against impossible odds or bad luck. There are a host of words in our language that you should concentrate on eliminating from your daily thoughts; words like *"can't, impossible, hopeless and futile."* They carry a negative connotation that will work ardently against your success unless you eradicate them from your conscious thought. Even the word *"luck"* denotes the existence of something that we have considerable difficulty defining. The reason for that is because it really does not exist. Everything in our lives happens for a reason. Although we don't always realize it, there are thoughts in our minds that actually bring about what happens to us, and luck has nothing to do with it.

More often than not, our desire to give up emanates from a lack of self-confidence or self-esteem. Self-confidence grows with successful accomplishments, even if only small ones, building one on top of another.

A sales achiever accepts the responsibility to make it happen, no matter what it takes. We can learn from a baby who, when learning to walk, persists until he or she learns to walk.

When was the last time you heard of someone who became too frustrated learning to walk as a child, and decided to crawl for the rest of their life? Obviously, it doesn't happen, but some people have less sense than a baby. They approach a task with an *"I'll try"* attitude.

The word *"try"* is really an invalid word. Let me give you an example. Try to pick up a chair. Grab hold of the chair and try to lift it. I said, just try. Now, you are probably thinking, *"How do I carry out the act of trying without actually lifting the chair?"* You see, you can't. In reality, you either lift the chair or you don't. There is no such thing as trying to lift the chair. It's one or the other. Catch yourself the next time you hear that word come from your mouth. Either commit or don't. There is no in-between.

In the movie *Star Wars*, Yoda asked Luke Skywalker to commit to winning the battle with the force of darkness, Darth Vader. Luke said, *"I will try."* Yoda responded with *"Luke, either you do or do not, there is no try."*

Persist until you achieve your results, and believe that the world is on your side, because it is. Don't allow fear of failure to immobilize you. Fear is a movement of your mind which creates what you expect.

> *What You Fear, You Will Attract,*
> *And What You Experience Is What You Expect*

We can put fear of failure behind us by doing the things we fear. Do the things you fear and you will control fear. By refusing to back down, refusing to quit, and persisting in achieving your results, you will succeed.

When you are feeling down and ready to quit, step back and take another look at your situation for a moment; view it from the point of a challenge. What you are attempting may not be that conventional, but you must challenge the conventional in order to succeed. You need perseverance to do as you dream. You must have an unreasonable passion – virtually an obsession – for being your best. After all, an obsession is the persistent, disturbing preoccupation with an often unreasonable idea. Break away from convention and you will be amazed at how you will always attract all the help you need.

NEVER TURN AGAINST YOURSELF DURING TOUGH TIMES

The reality of life is that things don't always go perfectly for all of us, all the time; accomplishing our goals can entail a lot of hard work and difficulties. That's what being human is all about, and it's perfectly normal.

The important thing is to never put yourself down in such situations and to maintain – even reinforce – a strong, positive attitude. Perseverance is one of the most important principles until you eventually get yourself back on the right track. If you use up your energy fighting yourself, you won't have any left to battle your opponent. That opponent may be anything from a particular person, as in a sport, to overcoming something you find particularly difficult.

BE PREPARED MENTALLY

No athlete expects to enter a competition without first having spent considerable time and energy in practice. The same applies to whatever you want to do in attaining your goal. Contrary to common belief, practice should encompass about ten percent physical effort and ninety percent mental preparation. Do whatever is necessary to get your mind focused. Practice with the same intensity and emotional commitment that you'll generate in the real situation.

You must occasionally take on the role of a spectator for a moment, step outside of yourself and look at yourself and your behavior. Napoleon Hill called this intelligent objectivity. This process will give you a brief break in the intensity, permit you to recharge your batteries with ever-expanding energy and enable you to re-enter the process more intensely. The process of retaining perspective on your activities is a very powerful tool for managing stress and maintaining emotional balance.

At this point I want to repeat the statement we began this lesson with, and I would like you to repeat it to yourself over and over again until it becomes like a tune, a favorite tune, a song that you keep playing over and over again in your mind. By doing this you will turn responsibility into a habit and you'll never catch yourself in the dumb blame game that losers keep practicing.

> "I take complete and absolute responsibility for the results that I experience in all aspects of my life. Because I know I am responsible for what comes into my life, I daily train my mind to view everything that happens to me, for me or around me as a lesson."

"THE DESTINY OF MAN IS
IN HIS OWN SOUL."

– HERODOTUS, GREEK HISTORIAN.
484 – C.420 BC.

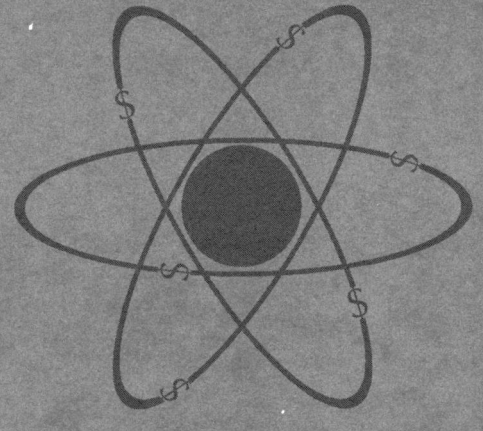

CHAPTER 5

LEARNING

DNA STRAND 4:
LEARNING

"In times of change, learners inherit the earth, while the learned find themselves beautifully equipped to deal with a world that no longer exists."

– Hoffer

Contrary to popular belief, there is no such thing as an educated person. You are either learning or you are not. In today's world, it is vitally important that you see the truth in Eric Hoffer's statement. The win or loss, which is waiting in the wings for every person, is enormous. You get to choose which you will experience.

Examine what Mr. Hoffer said. There are two obvious parts to his statement. The first part is very clear; how well it is understood is another subject.

> *"The learners will inherit the earth."*

That's pretty straightforward. I want to come back and elaborate on that statement because it is exciting, full of promise and possibility. However it would probably be wise to look at the second part of his advice first. Then, if you happen to fall into the category Eric Hoffer referred to, you can change your situation and win.

> *"The learned find themselves beautifully equipped to deal with a world that no longer exists."*

In virtually every country of the world you can find individuals, thousands of them, walking the streets with degrees in their hands… degrees from prestigious universities. They cannot find work. Why? These individuals view the conditions and circumstances that surround them as very frightening. They are the people who Eric Hoffer referred to who *"are beautifully equipped to deal with a world that no longer exists."*

Look around. The world is definitely changing, and it will never be the same again. Power is slipping away, disappearing from some circles, and reappearing in others. Countries, companies and individuals who have held the power in the past are quickly losing it, if in fact they have not already watched it melt in their hands. Their often smug, sometimes selfish, domineering, complacent attitude has cost them dearly. They are confused and this confusion is frequently fueled by their own ignorance. When that happens it ultimately leads to anger or resentment – sometimes both. This negative energy is then quite frequently misdirected, possibly at their loved ones, which then causes an entire new set of problems.

These people are clutched by an unseen enemy and their frustration is endless because they are not sure what has happened or what is happening. Their world seems to be turning upside down.

The entire world is in the midst of a paradigm shift, which is unprecedented. There have been transitions in the past but nothing to equal what we are presently experiencing. The world is moving from an intellectual to a spiritual vibration. The rules for winning have changed dramatically and the majority of the populations are still living with the old rules. There are an enormous number of people in every community who have worked hard and disciplined themselves to follow the only rules they know… still they are losing. They are bewildered, confused and in many cases, angry and most feel their anger is justified, whether it is or not matters little. They are doing what they were taught by their parents, teachers, and employers. Unfortunately they too, were working with the old rules.

In the past, individuals were recognized and rewarded for what they knew. Corporations waited on the sidelines dangling monetary rewards attempting to attract the graduates from the big name universities of the world. There were the multi-million dollar MBA management development programs that corporations placed their hope in for years. Most everyone was conditioned to deify the intellect. Individuals were not properly recognized and rewarded for what they did.

Rather than focusing on what is or was wrong, we should let it go. Let the dead bury the dead. The world I grew up in is gone, forever. The world has changed. We live in the new era. This is a spiritual world governed by exact laws. Everyone who studies these laws and incorporates them into every aspect of their life will be richly rewarded. I believe we would be wise to go back to the promise Eric Hoffer shared, *"In times of change, the learners inherit the earth."*

The learners are continually preparing themselves to adapt to the changes. Rather than reacting, they are responding to these changes and they are responding in an appropriate manner.

The learners are excited with the prospects of what this paradigm shift is bringing.

"Greatness is developed by doing little things in a great way, every day." In 1903 Wallace D. Wattles shared that wisdom with us in a book he wrote on Greatness. I agree with Wattles. I also believe it helps if you are exposed to great teachers along the way.

Napoleon Hill wrote that it pays to know where to buy knowledge.

When it comes to teachers I have had the best. First I have had my own husband, Bob Proctor. I have observed first hand his vision… his persistence… his work ethic and most of all… his kind, generous and fair nature with everyone. As well, in business… mine and Bob's, I have worked with, mentored under and observed some of the best. To my good fortune, being around… working with… being exposed to these great individuals instilled in me a desire to be all that I can be!

You are a spiritual being living in a physical body. You have been blessed with intellectual factors which, when properly utilized, give you awesome power. You have infinite potential. There is no limit to what you are capable of doing. All things are possible.

I think it is easy to become enthusiastic in today's world. The opportunities that surround you and me are so exciting and so vast in numbers, our real problem seems to be deciding which of the opportunities we will be involved with first. If you have not surrounded yourself with individuals and opportunities that excite and motivate you… decide right now to change that.

I am in my own business with the greatest people in the world and I invite you to join me. **linda@lindaproctor.com**

"THE UNEXAMINED LIFE IS
NOT WORTH LIVING."

– SOCRATES, GREEK PHILOSOPHER
469 – 399 BC.

CHAPTER 6

SELF-DISCIPLINE

DNA STRAND 5:
SELF-DISCIPLINE

Turning Yourself On To Self-Discipline

STRATEGY 1:
MASTER YOUR HABITS.

Controlling Bad Habits – That statement is both true and false. True in the sense that before we know it, something that we thought we could easily master or control, is now much more difficult. It is a false statement because I do not believe any habit is unbreakable. Every habit can be subjected to our control. Controlling bad habits leads the list for ways to save time.

Show me any person with a strong sense of self-control and I'll show you a winner. Conversely a loser has little control.

The really high achievers in life have a common denominator – they have mastered their habits. Take a look for a minute at the really poor achievers in life; the opposite is true of them. The under achievers have failed miserably because they lack self-discipline. They always let things slip. They don't seem to have given enough attention and concern for the important things in life.

These people seem to have chosen the path of least resistance. They tried to take the easy way out because it meant less work on the hard things in life, namely change and control - me! Who are the most productive and successful people you know? Would they be characterized as people who have mastered habits? Are they highly disciplined people? How many people do you really know whom you would give the label – *"Highly disciplined"*? Can you name ten? Five? Two?

DELAYED GRATIFICATION

Delayed gratification can be defined as the delaying of the reward or pleasure phase and counting on, even scheduling of the investment or problem phase first to more fully enjoy the benefits later. It's getting the unpleasant task done first to enjoy the gratification more deeply later.

How far would Wayne Gretzky get if he tried to put the blessing or victory phase before the *"workout"* or investment phase? When the game came he wouldn't go very far without the early morning runs and late night practices. There's no way he could handle the game without delaying certain pleasures to more fully enjoy the victory phase later.

Delayed gratification means working on problems NOW. It may be tough, sure, it will be stretching; but you agree that for you to really enjoy the pleasure or payoff phase, you will work hard first. You forgo now so you can reap later.

Strategy 2:
Make a list of all the habits you would like to change in the next 2 years.

If you are as most people, you are probably wishing you were more disciplined. Many times a day, you might think critically of yourself for postponing (sometimes indefinitely!) those things that you know you want to change. There are certain things you know you should stop doing, yet you never seem to tackle it. There are certain other habits you know you should start doing, but have failed to begin.

The psychological cost for people is far too great to be living in that vast wasteland called, *"Lack of Discipline."* You know exactly what you need to do. For some reason, perhaps lack of motivation, lack of initiative or not having a plan, you have permitted yourself and your life to become cluttered with undesirable habits. The time to change all that is now!

Strategy 3:
Follow the 6-Step Process for developing Discipline in your life.

Step 1:
Identify one habit or area you would like to become more disciplined in.

The first step is to identify one specific behavior you would like to change. It should be written in behavior style. It should describe something you do now, that you would like to stop doing, or something you don't consistently do now, and would like to do regularly.

You can use this step to describe the outcome you would like to accomplish. You must however, confine each worksheet to one specific issue or behavior. Attempting to do too much may be discouraging. Each worksheet will take you through this 6 Step process. It only applies to one issue per worksheet.

STEP 2:
Find role models.

Ask yourself, *"Who is doing it right?"* By identifying one or more people who have discipline in this area you will see that if others can do it so can you.

The people you list in this section need not be personal acquaintances of yours. You may not know them personally at all. They may be alive or dead. The point here is to cause you to think about specific people whom you believe had control in this area. People you will emulate.

STEP 3:
List the benefits of becoming self-disciplined in this area.

Now ask yourself, *"What's in it for me?"* You want to consider why you want to develop in this area. By listing the rewards, you will be willing to work harder. You need to feel, smell, taste, see and touch exactly what it will be once you are strong in this area.

What this step does is gets you to focus on the benefits of becoming disciplined in this area. You could consider listing the pain of NOT becoming disciplined here.

STEP 4:
Consider the danger zones.

You now need to consider where you might fall. You need to give some thought to the danger zones. You know that if you are going to become more disciplined you will be tempted to fall off the wagon, to be led astray, to procrastinate. If you have been attempting to become more self-disciplined for some time, you know that for you there is a pattern of failure to comply. What happens for you? You start off strongly then before you know it, you are doing the very things you said you wouldn't, or you stopped doing the things you said you would and know you should.

List all the potential times, situations and areas that may cause you to fall, and then list how you will handle it. If you know that on business trips you eat too much, this is a danger zone. By acknowledging it, you can plan on how to handle it.

STEP 5:
Use Advanced Decision Making.

You cannot win in life if you are controlled by whimsical or situational decision-making. If you are to succeed in life, you will need to consider in advance, how you will live your life.

In this step you will need to give some thought to what specific actions you will need to take to accomplish the goal listed in Step 1. For example, if you wanted to become more disciplined in the area of exercise, one decision made in advance could be a decision to exercise for 45 minutes every morning upon waking.

You decide in advance that you will do this. You don't wait until the morning to see if you *"feel"* like doing it. You have already decided in advance how you will live your life.

Wayne Gretzky, the hockey superstar, did not decide every morning if he *"felt"* like practicing. No way. He got up to practice every morning at 4 a.m. and 5 a.m. He did so because he had decided in advance that if he was to become the world's greatest hockey player he would have to practice.

He got up because he thought the investment was worth it. He did not wait to see if he felt like practicing. When the alarm went off, he got up because that's what he (and his dad) decided in advance he would do.

STEP 6:
Enroll a support team.

This step is by far one of the most crucial. If you don't do this step, you are cheating yourself out of the real power behind this system. It is vital for you to finally becoming the strong and self-disciplined person you know you can and should be. Resist the temptation to avoid this step because it may be different from what you are used to or even comfortable doing. It will literally change your life.

What this step asks you to do is enlist the assistance of someone you respect to help you become disciplined in this area. Here's what you do. First, you need to think of someone whom you respect and someone who will be strong enough to hold you to certain decisions about becoming disciplined. You call this person and tell them that you have identified certain areas you are looking to becoming more disciplined in. You are going to

send them a copy of the worksheet and you would like them to hold you accountable to the actions and decisions on the sheet.

What this will do is force you to do what you said you would and know you should. Find someone to call you at least once a week. Allow yourself to become accountable to this person. This step has literally transformed my life.

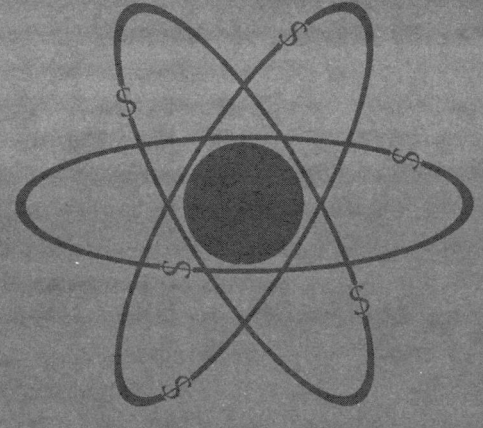

CHAPTER 7

RISK

DNA STRAND 6:
RISK

> ### Risk - It!

In 1925 there was a man in Indianapolis, Indiana in the United States of America, by the name of Herman Krannert, an executive of the Sefton Container Company. On one occasion he was summoned to Chicago to have lunch with the president of the company. He was very excited, because he had never been invited to do that before. He came to Chicago, went to the Athletic Club, and while they were having lunch, the president said, *"Herman, I'm going to make an announcement in the company this afternoon that greatly impacts your life. We're going to promote you to senior executive vice-president, and you're to be the newest member of the Board of Directors."*

Krannert was blown away. He said, *"Mr. President, I had no idea I was even being considered for this. I want you to know I'll be the most loyal employee this company has ever had. I'm going to dedicate my life to making this the finest corporation in America."*

The president was gratified by this and said, *"You know, Herman, I'm glad you mention that because there's one thing I'd like you to remember. As a member of the Board of Directors you will vote exactly the way I tell you to."*

That took the wind out of Krannert's sails, and he said he wasn't sure he could do that.

"Come on, Herman, that's the way it is in the business world. I'm putting you on the Board of Directors. You'll do what I tell you. Right?"

The more he thought about that, the angrier he became. At the end of lunch he stood up and said, *"Mr. President, I need you to understand I cannot accept this promotion. I will not be a puppet for anybody on a Board of Directors."* Then he added, *"Not only that, but I won't work for a company where such demands are made. I quit."*

He came back to Indianapolis that night, approached his wife, and said, *"You'll be excited to know that today I was promoted to senior executive vice-president, made a member of the Board of Directors, and I quit."*

She said, *"You quit? Have you lost you mind?"*

However, when he told her what had happened, she was very supportive and said, *"Well, I guess we'll have to find something else."*

Four nights later a knock came at his door. Six senior executives from his company burst through the door, all excited. *"Herman, we heard what happened the other day. We think that's the greatest thing we've ever heard. In fact, we quit too."*

"What do you mean, you quit too?" he said.

"Yeah, we quit too, and here's the good news. We're going to go to work for you!"

"How are you going to work for me? I don't even have a job."

They said, *"Oh, we figure you'll find something, and when you do we're going to work for you."*

That night those seven people sat down at Herman Krannert's dining room table and created the *Inland Container Corporation*. That empire exists today because a guy in 1925 knew what he believed in and decided to take a risk.

You got it. Through examples like this one of Herman Krannert and others I am going to share, I want to sell you on the idea of risk taking. I want to examine why it's important to be open to risk; to understand why it is so difficult for some people to leave the security of their *"comfort zone"* and I will provide practical suggestions on how you can continue to win big in life by taking risks.

If you are unwilling to risk, you are voting for mediocrity in your life. Let me first bring your attention to these risk takers:

When slavery was an accepted way to treat people, William Wilberforce stood up in the British Parliament, spoke out against it, and began the process of abolishing it. Wilberforce was willing to risk. Think about what it took.

When Rosa Parks refused to go to the back of the bus as was the custom for Black people, she risked and won. She ignited the Civil Rights movement in the United States.

When Colonel Sanders refused retirement and founded Kentucky Fried Chicken at the age of 65, he showed he was a risk taker.

When the Singaporean government caned teenager Michael Fay for vandalism in the face of world wide pressure, they took a risk.

Risk can be costly. It can be dangerous. You need to really think.

Canadian Robert Campeau put everything on the line to finance his enormous retail ventures in the United States and lost his fortune.

Billions were lost in the USA during the failed Savings & Loans scandals.

Fortunes vanished instantly on October 19, 1989, when the stock market collapsed. Had people considered the risk? Were they prepared?

I personally left a comfortable six figure income to take a ground breaking position with a new company and I won in a big way. If you are ready to make it in a big way contact me immediately. You are the kind of person I want to help become wealthy. **linda@lindaproctor.com**

"FORTUNE FAVORS
THE BRAVE."

– VIRGIL, ROMAN POET
70 – 19 A.D.

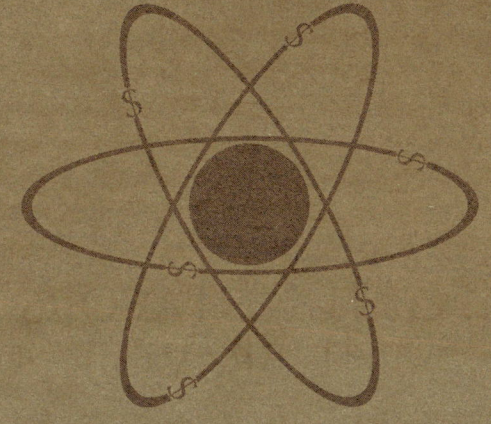

CHAPTER 8

ACTION

DNA STRAND 7:

ACTION

Action is a great word, isn't it? If you were thinking of words that were motivational, Action would have to be near the top of the list. In the lines to follow, I want to add new meaning to this power word for your benefit.

In a movie or play you will hear the director calling for *"Action."* The cameras begin to roll and things begin to happen. Used in the context of war, Action can have a very negative sting. You frequently hear of individuals being wounded or *"killed in action."*

In this book, action is being used as a very positive power principle. I want the concept of Action to play a positive role in your life. My *Webster's Dictionary* has a number of different meanings for the word Action. *"The process of doing."* That is the definition on which most people would focus their attention.

I want to suggest you put a different twist on the word Action. Make it a principle which gives you power. Make a decision to develop a reputation of being a person of outrageous Action; a person who makes the important moves, a person who gets the big things done.

When you want to go on a vacation, make it worthwhile. GO AROUND THE WORLD. Explore a country and visit a culture on the other side of the globe. Make the trip a memorable one. If the Action is to improve your business, DOUBLE OR POSSIBLY TRIPLE your business. When you call for Action, make it explosive Action, so that the big moves are not something in which other people are always involved.

Goethe, the German philosopher, has been quoted as saying, *"Before you can DO something, you must first BE something."* And of course Goethe is right. Doing is the expression of what has already taken place mentally. It is the expression of an impression. Action and doing are synonymous when they are used in this context. However, the word Action adds an explosive dimension to the process of doing.

Think about it for a moment. If I had titled this article Doing, it would have sounded weak when compared to Action. Action is definitely a power word. When you move into Action on an idea, you are involved in the final stages of creation, insofar as that idea is concerned. Action is not something that should be focused on or forced. Action should be automatic. Keep in mind, Action is the physical expression of a higher activity.

> ACTION IS THE EXPRESSION OF AN IMPRESSION. WHEN YOU GET EMOTIONALLY INVOLVED WITH YOUR BIG IDEAS, THE ACTION BECOMES AUTOMATIC. YOU WILL NOT BE ABLE TO STOP IT.

"Ideas are like slippery fish. If you don't gaff them with the point of a pencil, they will probably get away and might never come back."

– Earl Nightingale

Over the past years, experience has taught me many lessons. I have come to the conclusion that, as a people, we are far too regimented in our behavior.

Here is another point you might want to consider. When the time arrives for the birth to take place, the only people the mother wants in her life at that particular time are those people who are capable, competent and who want to give their undivided attention to assisting in the birth of her child. Long after the child has been safely delivered and mom is completely rested from her flurry or creative activity, a little idle chatter with a few non-productive, possibly scatterbrained acquaintances or relatives, would probably be allowed. Even then, almost everyone's attention is attracted back to the magnificence of the newly arrived creation. New creation generally attracts almost everyone's attention and admiration. The supreme satisfaction, which many people miss out on in life, comes only to those main contributors who work in harmony with the Creator for the physical manifestation of the new creation. I have always felt that a mother receives a degree of satisfaction, which the father will never completely understand, as her contribution in the birth of the child is so much greater than that of the father.

Now let's move back to the explosive word Action. You want to be recognized as a person of Action… I'm sure you do. You are a creative expression of life. You have been endowed with the mental tools that enable you to work in harmony with the ever present, all-powerful, all knowing Creator. So far as we know, you are the only form of life which has been given these marvelous mental powers. The nucleus of your being is creative; it is perfect. It is always longing for expansion and fuller expression. You are capable of, and designed to do, great work. You were never meant to spend your days involved in idle chatter or meaningless activity. It is your responsibility to grow… to develop a greater awareness… to enjoy every good imagined. If you haven't already got a dynamite idea running around your mind, adding dimensions of joy and enthusiasm to your days… quit whatever you are doing… lay back… relax and permit your imagination to move freely. Begin to look from within to your source of unlimited supply. Look at your work. How can you improve what you are doing… how can you make it 10 times, even 50 times better? Don't worry about getting paid for it… that will come, it must come, and that is the law. Write your ideas down as they come to you.

> ACTION IS THE EXPRESSION OF AN IMPRESSION. WHEN YOU MENTALLY WORK ON YOUR BIG IDEAS, THE ACTION BECOMES AUTOMATIC. YOU WILL NOT BE ABLE TO STOP IT.

When you are mentally pregnant with a big idea keep this idea in mind; Action comes when the idea is ready, not when the clock dictates. Have you ever noticed that the real professionals in every walk of life are not clock-watchers? Nor are they controlled or guided by the dictates of the masses. When they are ready for Action, they act.

The birth of ideas and the birth of babies are governed by exactly the same laws. Examine what I have just shared with you… think… really think. There is only one all knowing, creative power in this universe. This power expresses itself in many ways, but it always works the same way… by law. Every form of creation is by law.

When a woman is carrying a baby in her womb, she is referred to as being pregnant with a new child. To make certain she carries the baby to full term and a healthy birth, there are certain rules that must be followed. Rest, relaxation, physical

exercise, freedom from worry or stress, proper diet, and nutrition are all considerations to which a responsible mother gives high priority. And, let's keep this basic truth in mind: when the time for the birth of the baby arrives, nothing, absolutely nothing, but the birth, receives mom's attention. I should probably add complete and undivided attention. You just try and get her to go back to sleep or watch T.V. You know how successful you would be.

Neither conditions nor circumstances should prevent you from creating, and acting on your creations. Remember that Action is the final stage of creation. The creation and Action is continuous; it keeps going.

Positive Action is preceded by emotional involvement. Build the image and keep thinking about it. Continually give it the energy it requires to sustain life. You are probably aware that millions of ideas are either aborted prior to birth or are stillborn. Negative suggestions from ignorant, but well-meaning people, coupled with doubt, worry, and possibly envy are generally what take the life out of most great ideas. Just as the expectant mother must care for the unborn child she carries, you must care for the unborn idea you carry. Associate with positive thinking people.

Henry David Thoreau said, *"If a person will move confidently in the direction of their dream... and endeavor to live the life they have imagined... they will meet with success unexpected in common hours."* Thoreau was right. Mentally look after the idea and one day, it will just happen.

Action is the expression of an impression. When you get emotionally involved with your big ideas, the Action becomes automatic. You will not be able to stop it. The Action comes through you, which causes re-action. The re-action comes from the universe. The action meeting the re-action alters your conditions, circumstances and environment that produce your result – your creation.

Permit me to share a wonderful story with you. It's a
true story that happened to some very nice people in Northern
Ontario, Canada. The story is about a dirt-poor prospector who,
day after day, month after month, year after year, would leave his
home and his family to go prospecting for gold. There were times
when they had next to nothing to eat. Whenever this man's wife
or son voiced concern about the future, the man would assure
them they need not worry; they had wonderful times coming
when he found his gold mine. He was a man of great faith, but
he was also a man of Action. He imagined himself with a gold
mine and he would continually move into Action, always out
looking for it. He was a prospector.

> EVERY MOVEMENT IN WHICH YOU ENGAGE
> IN IS AN ACTION. ACTION IS SOMETHING IN
> WHICH YOU ARE ALREADY INVOLVED. THE
> TRICK IN LIFE IS TO CONTROL AND DIRECT
> THE ACTION, WHICH WILL EVENTUALLY
> CAUSE YOU TO FIND YOUR GOLD MINE.

It was the week between Christmas and New Year's Day.
At that time of year in Northern Ontario in Canada, the snow
is several feet deep and it is bitterly cold. It is predominantly a
Christian community, so being Christmas, very few people work.
Most folks lay around at home. It is a time to be with the family.
Although I have not checked this out, I feel fairly safe in saying
there were babies born that week in that cold, snow swept town.
The babies didn't care what the occasion was or what the weather
was like; the time had elapsed and the baby arrived; mom gave
birth.

Well, the time also arrived for this man's idea to be acted
upon. No one prospected for gold in this area between Christmas

and New Year's Day. Anyone who did, or even suggest they would, were considered to be insane. Nevertheless, this poor prospector called his partner and said, *"It's time, we must go."* Something inside of him caused him to move into Action. So off they went, just outside of town. The snow was so deep they were only able to venture a few feet off the main highway. Standing a few feet off the main road in freezing temperatures and deep snow, the poor prospector said, *"This is the place."* They went far beyond what any right-minded gold prospector would consider suitable with their drilling. However, it was at that very place between Christmas and New Year's Day that the poor prospector and his partner became extremely wealthy, multi-million dollar owners of the Hemlow Gold Mines.

It was at dinner one evening that Paul Larch, who is a friend of Bob's, shared that story with him. You see, the poor prospector who became the wealthy owner of the Hemlow Gold Mines is John Larch, Paul's father. They are good, decent people. If you met them, I know you would be happy it happened to them. Paul told Bob he just knew his dad would find a gold mine. He knew it because his dad kept telling him he would, from the time he was a little boy, and as Paul said, *"Dad believed he would."* It was that belief over the years that fueled the idea, the image. He impressed such great energy upon his subconscious mind for so long, he moved himself into the vibration he had to be in, to attract what he attracted. The image within John Larch became so explosive it had to be acted upon. Christmas… cold… snow… none of that mattered. He had to move into Action on the idea. The Action was automatic. It was the expression of the impression.

Do you have an idea big enough to keep you enthusiastic for years? John Larch did. A benefit that came to John as a result of the gold mine is the faith he instilled in his son Paul… the *"can do"* attitude with which Paul was raised. John Larch was a very rich man before he ever struck gold... he had, and gave his son, what no amount of gold could ever buy.

Adjust your thinking... if it is on the wrong track fix it. Remember this: *"What you don't fix... your children will inherit."*

It seems to be fairly easy for a person to believe that great things can happen to others, but not to them. If you are caught in this trap, I suggest that you analyze the creative process. You will see that you have the tools for greatness. Although these people came from varied backgrounds, there is one factor which remained constant and that was the creative process which produced the results in their lives. Their results were preceded by an Action, which was automatic. It was the expression of the thought and ideas, which had been impressed upon their emotional mind over a period of time. They became what they thought about. The thought always propels Action.

You see the bottom lines are obvious when you really think about it. That is what all the big producers do.

You are like the great people you read about. Take Action, go, and meet them. The more of these people you get to know, the more you will see that you are like them, and the better you will feel about yourself. The better you feel about yourself, the more confident you will become. The more confident you become, the easier it will be for you to move into Action on your big ideas and to solve the inherent problems that come with them.

"When we feel confident about ourselves, we know we can solve the problems, or at least put them into perspective and remind ourselves of our abilities when things aren't going well."

Don't worry about what might happen when you explode into Action on your big idea. Whatever happens will be what must happen for your idea to move into its final form of creation… the physical form… which is always your result.

And permit me to make one more offer… if you want to begin spending more time with Action Oriented individuals let me know. **linda@lindaproctor.com**

CONCLUSION

As your eyes traveled across each page you gathered information that has literally transformed my life and hopefully will do the same for you. Strange as it may seem, I had read much of this information before I met Bob Proctor but obviously never acted on the information. Bob showed me how to implement ideas and the strategy he used was definitely transformational. He also asked me to make a commitment to share what I had learned with as many people as possible. He said money, or the lack of it, causes enormous problems in people's lives. I committed to him to share this with everyone with whom I work. And I am prepared to show you how to do what I have done.

Bob Proctor often talks in his seminars about people making a decision to turn their annual income into a monthly income. I am pleased to tell you, I have been able to do better than that. At various places in the book I invited you to contact me. One last time I would like to repeat that offer. If you sincerely desire to multiply your income… truly enjoy time and money freedom, send me an e-mail and I will get back to you. **Linda@lindaproctor.com**

You Were Born Rich

Bob Proctor
ISBN # 978-0-9656264-1-5

The Millionaire Mindset
How Ordinary People Can Create Extraordinary Income

Gerry Robert
ISBN # 978-1-59930-030-6

Rekindle The Magic In Your Relationship
Making Love Work

Anita Jackson
ISBN # 978-1-59930-041-2

Finding The Bloom of The Cactus Generation
Improving the quality of life for Seniors

Maggie Walters
ISBN # 978-1-59930-011-5

The Beverly Hills Shape
The Truth About Plastic Surgery

Dr. Stuart Linder
ISBN # 978-1-59930-049-8

Wellness Our Birthright
How to give a baby the best start in life.

Vivien Clere Green
ISBN # 978-1-59930-020-7

Lighten Your Load

Peter Field
ISBN # 978-1-59930-000-9

Change & How To Survive In The New Economy
7 steps to finding freedom & escaping the rat race

Barrie Day
ISBN # 978-1-59930-015-3